TRANSITION

For every emotion
that is asked to be
seen

~Meenaakshi Sunil

TRANSITION

ISBN – 978 - 93 – 5592 – 372 – 1

Published by Meenaakshi Sunil

Postal Code: 201016

Crossings Republik, Ghaziabad,

Uttar Pradesh, India

Cover design: Canva

Dedicated to

YOU

FOREWORD

I didn't write this book because I had all the answers. I wrote it because I needed to say the things I wished someone had told me when I felt small, unseen, or like a burden. I wrote it for the moments when the world feels too loud, too fast, or too heavy—and for the moments when the world feels completely silent, leaving only your thoughts to echo.

This book is a collection of reflections, whispers, and truths that helped me feel a little lighter, a little more seen, a little more whole. It's messy, imperfect, and deeply personal—because life is messy, imperfect, and deeply personal. It's not a guide, a set of rules, or a plan to "fix" anything. It's a companion, a hand extended in quiet understanding.

If you've ever doubted your worth, if you've ever felt like your emotions were "too much," or if you've ever questioned whether you matter—these pages are for you. They are for anyone who has felt unseen, unheard, or like their presence is a burden. They are a reminder that you do matter, and that your feelings are valid.

I wrote this book not just to share my experiences, but to remind both myself and others that healing is not linear, self-love is not perfect, and being enough is not something we earn—it is who we already are. Some days are harder than others, some days feel lighter, and some days feel like we're starting all over again. That's okay. That's human.

As you read these words, I hope you feel less alone. I hope you feel seen. I hope you feel reminded that it is possible to exist in your own skin, to honor your emotions, and to gently, quietly tell yourself: *I matter. I am enough. I am not a burden.*

This book is not a set of answers. It is a reflection of a journey—mine, yes, but also a mirror for anyone who has walked, or is walking, a similar path. May these words be a quiet companion, a reminder of resilience, and a gentle hand holding yours as you navigate your own journey.

Contents

"This is not a book of advice. These are the things I needed to hear when I was drowning in silence. Maybe you need them too."

ACKNOWLEDGEMENT

I want to start with my mom. Mom, thank you. Thank you for holding me, even when I felt too much or too small, even when life felt heavy and confusing. You taught me what quiet strength looks like, and you gave me love in ways words can't fully capture. You carried me through fears I couldn't name, and you still do. Every word in this book carries pieces of your love and patience, and I am endlessly grateful.

To my loved ones—my friends, my family, and those who stood by me when I was fragile—I see you. You offered your presence, your ears, your hearts, and your unwavering belief in me when I couldn't see it myself. You reminded me that I am not alone, that my emotions are valid, and that connection is sacred. Every laugh, every tear, every quiet moment of understanding helped me find myself again.

To the universe—I am humbled by your guidance and by the small miracles that showed up when I needed them most. Thank you for the synchronicities, the moments of clarity, and the unseen threads that brought people, experiences, and hope into my life.

To my younger self—thank you for surviving, for showing up even when it hurt, for learning to believe in yourself despite the doubts. Your courage made this book possible.

And finally, to you, the reader—thank you. Thank you for opening this book, for allowing these words into your life, and for letting them remind you that you are seen, you are heard, and you are never a burden. I hope this book offers the same comfort and reassurance that it gave me while writing it: that your feelings matter, your heart matters, and you matter.

From the depths of my heart, I am so happy, so grateful, and so full of love for all of you.

The pages turn, a little torn,
yet beauty blooms where I was worn.
No need for perfect, just to be—
I fly, I fall, I'm finally free.
Thank you, life, for all I've earned—
in every tear, a lesson learned.

~M. S

When You Feel Like a Burden

"You don't need to be loud to take up space.
You don't need to be broken to deserve love.
And you are never a burden — not now, not ever."

No one ever tells you that you're a burden. It's not something people say aloud. It's quieter than that — a belief you grow into without realizing. Especially if you grew up in a time or place where emotions were tucked away, hidden behind smiles and small talk.

You start to feel it everywhere. Every day. Every night. You whisper it to yourself — softly, but constantly. You pull back. You isolate. You convince yourself that independence is strength, that needing help makes you weak. You stop sharing what hurts because you're terrified of being "too much."

I've been there.
As a kid, I felt like I was always taking up too much space. I learned to shrink — to be quiet, to be helpful, to never need anything. No one told me I was a burden, but I carried the belief anyway. It shaped me. It fueled my need for perfection. It made me hyper-aware of everyone else's moods, constantly reading the room like my safety depended on it.

And in some ways, it did.
My relationship with my father wasn't just strained — it was toxic. Every step, every word, I walked on eggshells. One wrong move could set off an explosion. When my mom finally divorced him, I realized something: all that pain, all that fear, forced me to grow up faster than I

should have. I never wanted that lesson — but it made me resilient.

Still, the fear followed me into school. I doubted myself constantly. I couldn't raise my hand, couldn't ask questions, couldn't even show confusion — because I thought my uncertainty was an inconvenience. I thought *I* was an inconvenience.

Maybe you know that feeling too. Maybe someone — a parent, a friend, a teacher — made you feel like your emotions were "too much." Maybe you learned to hold everything in just to keep the peace.

But here's the truth:
You are not too much.
You are not too little.
You are *enough*.

Your worth isn't measured by how easy you are to love or how much you stay silent. It's in your heart, your growth, your resilience.

These days, I’m learning to believe in myself again — to remind myself that I am not a burden. Some days it’s easy. Some days it’s not. But I keep trying.

Try this: write it down somewhere.
“I am not a burden. I matter.”
Write it until it feels real.
Because it *is* real.

You are not a burden.
You matter. Always.

Reflection Space

"When you start believing you're not a burden, healing begins."

☐ What's one small way you can show yourself some care today?

What's something you've been afraid to ask for?

Affirmation:

I am not too much. I am not too little. I am enough.

Why silence is sometimes a scream?

"Sometimes silence isn't peace — it's exhaustion wearing a quiet face."

Your surroundings are quiet.
Not a single voice — just birds chirping, sunlight stretching across your face.
You sit on your balcony chair, sipping coffee, reading *Do It Today* by Darius Foroux.
You're trying to enjoy the moment, to focus... but your thoughts are loud.

They criticize you.
They make you self-conscious.
You try to block them out — reading word by word —
but nothing sinks in.
You sigh, reread the same line for the third time.

Then — the doorbell rings.

And suddenly, there's silence.
Not outside — inside.
Your mind freezes.
No more criticism. Just one thought:

Who is it?

You walk to the door.
A delivery man stands there, maybe in his forties or fifties —
impatient, tired.

And your thoughts begin again.

"He's annoyed by you."
"You're ugly."
"You made him wait."
"Why didn't you open the door faster?"

"Ma'am, your parcel."

You snap back.
Take the parcel. Close the door.
You don't open it. It's not even for you.

Back to the balcony.
You take a sip of coffee — it's gone cold.
And your mind starts screaming again.
But the world remains silent.

That’s the thing about silence —
it doesn’t always mean calm.
Sometimes it means chaos has found a
quieter way to exist.

People suffer in silence.
They may seem peaceful —
but inside, they’re fighting storms no
one can see.

You might not hear it.
You might not notice it.
So, please — be gentle.
Be kind.

Because you never really know
what volume someone’s mind is set to.

Reflection Space

"Recognizing your needs is not selfish- its self-respect."

☐ What is the One need of yours you often ignore?

How can you honor this need today in a small practical way?

Which thoughts or beliefs get in the way of asking for what you need?

Affirmation:

My needs are valid, and its safe for me to express them.

Always the Listener, Never the Talker

*"It's beautiful to be someone's safe space.
But you deserve one too."*

"You're such a good listener."
"Thank you for listening to me."

Pretty good compliments, right?
Yeah, I felt good hearing them too — for many years.
After all, they *were* compliments.

But deep down, I longed for someone to listen to *me*.
To sit quietly and just hear my problems, my happiness, my little stories.
I wished for it for so long... until one day, I stopped wishing.

Then, unexpectedly, I met someone who *wanted* to listen — genuinely.

Not out of politeness or obligation.
It wasn't casual; it was real.

I was stunned.
I didn't even know what to say.
Did I even have any stories to tell anymore?
I was so confused that I stumbled over my own words.
I couldn't express myself.

But thank God, he was patient with me.
He didn't judge.
He just *knew* I needed time — time to remember how to talk, how to share again.
Whenever I got lost in my thoughts, he would say,
"Just let it all out. I'll help you reorder them."

Sweet and romantic, right?
But for me, it was more than that — it was *healing.*
He was healing me without even realizing it.
But before him... who listened to me?

Blank pages.

My diary became my listener.
Every night, it was my silent therapy session — a space to vent, cry, and release.
Those pages had more patience than anyone I'd ever met.

Every listener needs their own listener, too.
They want to talk.
They want to express.
They want to be heard.

So, if you're a listener — be a talker, just for today.
No filters. No guilt. Let it all out.
Let the world know that you have your own universe inside you,
a world that's been quietly screaming to be known.

And remember — no judgment.
That's the most important part.

And if you can't find anyone to listen right now —

you’ve got me.
Write it all down.
You have your space here, sweetheart.

Reflection Space

"Boundaries are a form of self-love, not rejection."

☐ Which situation in your life challenges your boundaries the most?

How can you gently communicate a boundary this week?

What feelings arise when you think of saying 'no'?

Affirmation:

I can protect my energy with kindness and clarity.

I'm Not a Project. I'm a Person.

"You are not here to be fixed.
You are here to be felt, understood, and accepted — as you are."

If you're the eldest sibling — especially the eldest *daughter* — this chapter is for you.

There's a pressure no one prepares you for.
The pressure to be perfect.
To lead by example.
To score top marks.
To make your parents proud.
To take care of everyone and everything —
Just because you were born first.

You didn't ask for this role.
You didn't sign up to be a blueprint.
But somehow, you became the "project."
And if you fail in *just one* thing?

Boom.
Suddenly, you're flawed.
Suddenly, you're "selfish."
All because you chose *yourself.*

Being the eldest daughter came with its pros and cons...
But the thing that broke me the most?
The taunts.
The disappointment in their eyes when I failed.
The way they labeled me selfish for simply existing as a person with dreams, limits, and emotions.

Sometimes, I wish I were the youngest
—
Just so I could be treated like a person,
Not a project under construction.

Now that I think about it,
This isn't just a family dynamic.
It's *society's* expectation.
The eldest must be strong. Must succeed. Must be the adult even when they're still a child.

But the day I shattered that illusion —
The day I stopped chasing the "perfect daughter" fantasy —
Everything changed.

I started choosing myself.
I started breathing again.
I started listening to *my own* voice.

Of course, the world around me didn't applaud.
Everything changed… and not all of it was easy.

But here's what I learned:
I'm not here to be their project.
I'm not a checklist of accomplishments.
I'm a person.

And that's more than enough.

And I need you to be same too.
don't guilt yourself.
Your dreams matter.
Your voice matters.
You matter.
and that's it

Reflection Space

"Change is not a threat; it's an invitation to grow."

□ What recent change in your life felt challenging or uncomfortable?

How can you approach change with curiosity instead of fear?

What lessons has change taught you so far?

Affirmation:

I welcome change as
a path to growth
and self-discovery.

When You Don't Want to Get Better, Just Disappear

"Sometimes healing begins with vanishing —
not because you're weak,
but because it's the only way to hear your own voice again."

It's been three months since you started your Instagram account.
You're getting recognition, brand deals, free stuff, and money.
Every day you scroll to follow trends.
Every night you give your entire self to the feed.

Your screen time climbs from two hours to five, then seven, then ten, then fourteen... seventeen... nineteen.

You stop going out. No sunlight.
You don't even remember if you've eaten.

You're lying on your couch all day. No calls to friends. Isolation feels easier.

One day you can't even scroll anymore. You just want to cry — but the tears won't come. They've disappeared, as if they never existed.

You think, but about what? There's nothing left to think about.
You remember your fights with your mom, her criticism about you doing nothing. She was right, but you couldn't accept it.
Now every day blurs into the next: sleep, reels, nothing.

Months pass like this.

You look at your failures. You want to cry, but instead you pick up a notebook and pen.
You write what you're feeling.

One sentence comes out:
"I feel empty."

Tears finally fall on the page, making the ink bleed.
You realize it's been three months...

You stand up. You walk toward your balcony. You open the curtains and a ray of light hits your eyes.
You flinch at first, but then step closer.
You walk outside.
You breathe — a deep, long breath — and you try to show your smile lines to the world.

It's hard. It's so hard.
But you know if you go back inside, it's all black again.
Empty. No space for any emotion, not even sadness.

You pick up your phone.
You delete every video you've uploaded.
You delete every social app.

You disappear.

And in that moment, you realize you *do* want to get better. You're just not ready to show the world yet. You need time to convince yourself.

So, you disappear to be reborn — like a phoenix from your own ashes.

When you don't want to get better,
disappear.
Step away.
Touch the real world that exists both inside and outside you.
It might be the hardest thing you'll ever do.

But you can do it.

Reflection Space

"Strength grows in the moments when you think you can't go on, but you keep going anyway."

☐ When did you recently feel tested or stretched beyond your comfort zone?

What inner resources or strengths did you discover in yourself?

How can you nurture your resilience for the challenges ahead?

Affirmation:

I honor my inner strength and trust in my ability to overcome challenges.

The Friendship That Saved Me Quietly

"Some people don't save us with grand gestures —
they save us by simply showing up, again and again,
until we start showing up for ourselves."

"Hey... you don't call or text anymore. Is anything wrong? How are you?"

I cried hard that day.

After high school ended, I isolated myself completely. I disappeared—from friends, from life, from myself. I was ashamed of my failures, drowning in my own self-doubt and feeling like a complete mess. I just wanted to vanish.

Then, one day, like some quiet miracle, I picked up her call.
It had been more than three months since we last talked. I didn't plan to talk

long—I thought I'd just say I was "busy." But then she asked me something I hadn't heard in years:

"How are you?"

Was she talking to me?
That was my first thought.

I genuinely believed I had become invisible. That my existence didn't matter. That my emotions didn't matter. And yet, this human—someone I once even *resented* back in school—asked me that one question. And it broke me open.

We ended up talking for **two hours**. We shared our struggles. We laughed. We vented about our mutual enemies (every school has a few). I never thought a two-minute call would turn into a two-hour heart-to-heart. I didn't plan on being raw or vulnerable, but somehow, she made me feel safe.

She didn't try to fix me. She didn't offer any grand advice.

She just reminded me I wasn't alone.

And she said it so quietly, so gently… it hit harder than any motivational quote or loud pep talk ever could.

Since that day, we talk more often—honestly, openly. It's not about solving everything. It's just about being there.

"Do Exercise from Tomorrow Onwards."

Another moment that quietly saved me came from someone closer than I expected—my mom.

One evening, I went for a walk with her. Out of nowhere, I told her I was feeling… low. Depressed. Numb.

She didn't say much. She just replied: **"Do exercise from tomorrow onwards."**

I was confused. Annoyed, even.

But the next morning? She literally **dragged me out of bed** and made me do crunches.
I was like, *seriously? Who does this to their own child?!*

But now... I do it every morning. It's a habit.
That one tiny push made me step into the sunlight again—both literally and mentally. I didn't know I needed it, but I'm so thankful she gave it anyway.

Just like that, you might have someone in your life who helped you *quietly*.
A friend. A parent. A stranger.
Maybe someone you once resented, or misunderstood.
But now, you see it—how they showed up for you in the softest, smallest ways.

The quiet ones often save us the loudest.

Reflection Space

"Change is not something to fear, but something to grow with."

What changes have recently happened in your life?

How did you respond to these changes, and what did you learn from them?

What small steps can you take to embrace future changes more gracefully?

Affirmation:

I welcome change as a pathway to growth and new possibilities.

Healing is Ugly, Not Poetic

"Healing isn't made of sunsets, candles,
or perfect routines.
It's messy. It's lonely.
And it's the bravest thing you'll ever do."

Now you walk towards your healing journey. You already know how aesthetic it looks on social media—but is it really?

The answer to that question only exists if you try.
So, are you ready for the healing journey of your life?

When I first started, the first thought that came to my mind was:
"A therapist."
Yes... but did I have the money to even afford a single session? No.

I searched every day online until I found a first free session.
With all the courage I had, I booked it.

It actually went pretty well. In just one hour, I understood more about myself than I had in years.
I realized I had to talk—really talk—about my deepest feelings, fears, secrets, and traumas.

They weren't aesthetic. They weren't beautiful.
They were ugly.

I had to write everything down.
Every single thing I felt—my secrets, my pain, my trauma.

I reread it... and then I burned it.
Because it was evidence.
Evidence of why I had become the way I was.

It was painful to read.
To imagine the child version of me going through those memories... it broke me.
It was hard to forgive the people who

hurt me.
I held grudges.
I held deep, burning rage.
I bottled up every emotion I had, for years.

I told the therapist as much as I could in that single hour.

And then, all she said was:
"Try painting again."

"Painting?"
I realized it had been years since I touched my brushes.

That was the saddest part.
Painting had once been my favorite thing in the world.
I had collections of prizes from various competitions.

Where was I all these years?
Why haven't I painted in so long?

All these questions flooded in.

So, I decided.
I would paint.
And this time—**I'd paint my emotions.**

It came out pretty dark, to be honest...
but it was manageable.
That first painting taught me something:
I had *so much* bottled up inside me.

I started slow.
And I'm still on this pretty-ugly healing journey.

If you're starting yours, **start it on your own terms**.

Other people will help.
Some will push you.
Some will test your patience.

For me, my mom was always beside me—either silently or by yelling at me.
It's funny... but filled with love.

You might not find a support system right away.

But the most important thing is to
believe in yourself during the process.

It's a never-ending-ending journey.
You'll discover your bad sides, your good sides—even the average sides.
But you'll move on.
Time won't stop for you, but you'll grow through it.

So, start today.
Do the thing you've always been thinking about.
This might be the best time.

Accept that you are human—with flaws.
And that *is* the new definition of perfection.
Without your flaws, it wouldn't be **you**.

So…
Breathe. *(Are you?)*
Smile. *(Come on, where is that beautiful smile?)*
And hydrate. *(Drink that water.)*

Healing is ugly.
But it's real.
And it's uniquely yours.

Reflection Space

"Strength doesn't come from what you can do, it comes from overcoming the things you once thought you couldn't."

When have you felt your strongest in the face of a challenge?

What personal qualities helped you overcome difficult moments?

How can you nurture and grow your inner strength moving forward?

Affirmation:

I am resilient, capable, and stronger than I realize.

Unlearning Perfection

"Unlearning is an art, and we all keep the caliber to learn it, so unlearn something that doesn't align with you today"

From my childhood, I was Ms. Perfect. I always aimed for the perfect score, perfect discipline, perfect handwriting. My room had to be spotless. My projects had to be spotless. My teachers couldn't have a single complaint.

And I was driven to be perfect because I thought that's how I would earn love—from my parents, my friends, everyone. I gave everything I had. I pushed myself to the limit. It was all or nothing. If I didn't do it perfectly, I felt like I had failed completely.

At the time, I thought I was just being ambitious. But it wasn't ambition.
It was fear.

Fear of being seen as less.
Fear of being judged.
Fear that my worth was tied to how flawlessly I could perform.

Coming out of my final years of high school, I began to see the truth:
My perfectionism was never about striving for excellence—it was about earning love.

Deep down, I believed that if I just did everything right, maybe then I would be enough.
Maybe then I'd deserve affection, validation, and peace.

And I know I'm not alone in this.
Maybe you've been there too.
Or maybe you're still in that exhausting loop.

I know it's not easy to break free—but you have to try.
At least once, you have to look yourself in the mirror and say:

"I deserve love and affection without needing to prove myself."

Because ***perfection doesn't lead to peace—it leads to exhaustion.***

By the end of it, I was completely drained.
My results were worse than ever.
But more than that—I had no energy left to care.
I was done. Done trying to prove my worth.

And that's when it hit me:
I wasn't even doing what I loved anymore.
I was living for approval—not for joy.

So, I stopped.

I decided to just ***be****.*

I reminded myself:
Love is not something you earn.
It's something you receive—freely, without conditions.
It's meant to ***fill*** *you, not* ***drain*** *you.*

And if you're reading this, maybe you need that reminder too.

You don't have to chase perfection to be worthy of love or validation.
You already are.

Perfection is a myth that slowly empties you.
It makes you believe your value lies in your performance—
but your value lies in your being.

So, take a breath.
Let the pressure fall away.
Your messy, imperfect, real self is already enough.

*You are **perfect as you are**.*

Give yourself permission to rest.
To fail.
To try again.
To live softly.

You don't have to earn love through perfection.

You only need to remember:
You already deserve it.

Because you do.
You always have.

Reflection Space

"Change is not something to fear, but something to embrace as a path to growth."

🌀 What recent change in your life has taught you the most?

How did you adapt to this change, and what did you learn about yourself?

What changes would you like to welcome in the future to help you grow?

Affirmation:

I embrace change with courage, curiosity, and an open heart.

Learning to be okay with being "ENOUGH"

"Being "enough" isn't about meeting expectations —
it's about accepting the quiet power of who you already are."

Being okay with being enough is tough. Because even when you say it out loud — "I am enough" — your heart doesn't always believe it.

I still run toward acceptance.
Toward validation.
Toward proof that I'm doing something right.

I always thought my efforts weren't enough.
Every time I looked around, I saw people achieving one goal after another — people becoming millionaires at

seventeen,
people starting businesses, traveling,
posting "success stories."
And there I was... sitting on my couch,
scrolling through my phone,
fantasizing about trips I wished I could take —
with a bank balance close to zero.

I was just eighteen.
And I thought I was already lagging behind.

But later, I noticed something — even content creators, the ones who seemed to have it all,
felt the same way at twenty-five.
They, too, thought they were behind.

That realization hit me hard.
Because I understood then:
I wasn't lagging behind life.
I was just chasing ***validation*** *—*
not from others, but from a version of myself that only existed online.

I was running toward aesthetic pictures
that had hundreds of filters on them —
filters that made everyone look happier,
richer,
more fulfilled than they actually were.

I was happy for others, truly.
But deep down, I resented myself —
for being that "lazy teen" with hundreds
of dreams
and zero energy to chase them.

The next morning, something inside me
whispered, slow down.
Really, slow down.

So, I did.
I didn't touch my phone.
I didn't make a to-do list.
I just sat at my study table and opened
my journal.

And I wrote —
everything.
The emptiness.
The self-doubt.

The guilt.
The fear.

Every single thought that made me feel "less."

And for the first time in forever,
I didn't feel like I had to ***earn the right to breathe.***

I was just... enough.
As I was.
Without proof.
Without achievements.
Without pretending.

I didn't think about all the moments I wasn't enough.
I simply accepted this one —
where I was okay,
where I was still learning,
and that was enough.

Life isn't a race — it's a rhythm.
And sometimes, the bravest thing you can do
is stop running
and let yourself simply exist.

Because you are enough.
Right now.
Exactly as you are.

Reflection Space

'Strength doesn't come from what you can do, it comes from overcoming the things you once thought you couldn't."

When have you surprised yourself with your own strength?

What challenges have helped you grow stronger?

How can you use your inner strength to support yourself or others in the future?

Affirmation:

I am strong, resilient, and capable of overcoming any challenge.

Co-exists

"Life can make no sense and still be worth living"

I think about this sentence often. It sounds simple, almost obvious, but it holds a truth I've only recently begun to understand: life is full of contradictions, and somehow, they're all valid. Two things — even if they seem completely opposite — can co-exist.

You can feel happiness and still feel guilty about it.
You can let go of someone and still love them deeply.
You can be grateful for what you have and still long for more.
You can believe in yourself and still feel too tired to hope.
You can know your direction and still doubt every single step.

No one really tells you that. We grow up thinking we're supposed to feel one thing at a time — like joy or sadness, love or loss, clarity or confusion. But real life is messier than that. I spent years trying to make sense of what I was feeling, wondering if I was broken or wrong because I couldn't choose a single emotion. I thought if I was happy, I wasn't allowed to feel anything else.

I remember during my gap year, I took a trip to Dubai. It was a beautiful experience — the kind that makes you feel alive and curious again. I was surrounded by new places, new people, and a sense of adventure. I should've felt nothing but excitement, right? But I didn't. Along with the happiness, there was guilt. My classmates were starting college, sharing stories and photos from their new beginnings, and I was somewhere else — on a different path. I started questioning myself: *Should I be doing something more productive? Am I wasting time?*

But now I realize — it's okay. It was okay to be happy in that moment and still carry guilt. That doesn't make either emotion less real. They just... co-existed.

There have been other times too. Moments when I was angry at someone I loved, yet still wanted to protect them. Or times I felt completely exhausted, but had to keep showing up with a calm face. Or when I was deeply hurt, but still held space for compassion. Or the times I cried while holding a trophy.

These contradictions don't make us weak or confused — they make us human.

No one warns you about the emotional gray areas. Everyone talks about strength, positivity, confidence. But no one talks about the moments where you feel both brave and scared, both lost and grounded, both full and empty. And those moments, I've learned, are just as real as the others.

So, if you're ever feeling like you don't make sense — like your emotions contradict each other — remind yourself that it's okay. You're not broken. You're just learning how to carry different truths at the same time.

And that's what life is — a story that doesn't always line up neatly, but still deserves to be lived.

Reflection Space

"Life doesn't always make sense, and that's okay. Two truths can exist at the same time."

☐ When have you felt two opposing emotions at once?

How did holding both emotions change your perspective or actions?

What contradictions in your life can you allow yourself to embrace without judgment?

Affirmation:

I honor all of my emotions, and I am allowed to feel them fully, even when they coexist.

Letting go of old me

"Growth begins the moment you stop clinging to a version of yourself that no longer fits."

"You've changed."

I was honestly stunned when he said that to me.
We ended up talking for nearly two hours — about how much we've grown, how we're no longer the same 16-year-old school kids we used to be.

A lot happened in those two years after high school.
We evolved. We changed. We healed.
We let go of so many things that no longer aligned with who we were becoming.

I was no longer people-pleasing.
I didn't crave constant validation

anymore.
I had started enjoying my own company.
After many years, I felt alive.
And I realized — I wasn't holding onto my past self anymore.

I was letting go of grudges I held towards my younger self.
I was forgiving — not forgetting, but learning to soften.
I was slowing down.
I was learning to feel every emotion as it passed through me.
And for the first time, I was truly grateful.

This... this is what growth looks like.
That chapter was over.

I know many of you are still struggling to let go of certain chapters —
Maybe it's a depressive episode that won't loosen its grip.
Maybe it's the ex you still hold onto.
Or a toxic relationship that feels familiar, but keeps hurting you.

I won't pretend to have the answers.
Because the truth is — the decision to let go, to choose differently — that's yours.
You hold the power to change your story.

But I can promise you this:
Once you let go of the old you,
You'll feel lighter — like a morning breeze.
You might even breathe easier.
You'll smile — not because you're supposed to, but because you actually feel it.

It won't be performative.
It'll be real.

I hope you find peace in every version of you —
In every chapter yet to come.

Reflection Space

"Growth begins the moment you stop clinging to a version of yourself that no longer fits."

□ Which parts of your past self are you ready to let go of?

✵ What lessons have you learned from the version of yourself you're leaving behind?

How can embracing the present version of yourself help you move forward with more peace and freedom?

Affirmation:

I honor my past,
release what no
longer serves me,
and embrace the
growth of the
person I am
becoming.

Still figuring out

"It's okay to not have all the answers.
The journey itself is the answer."

You might think I have it all figured out...
but trust me,
I'm still learning how to love myself
without conditions.
Still figuring out how to be proud of
progress no one else can see.
Learning to stop measuring growth by
productivity alone.
Trying to exist softly, without needing to
prove I deserve to.

I'm still working on forgiveness —
especially for myself.
Still learning how to rest.
Still realizing that peace doesn't always
look like joy —
Sometimes it's just the silence that
doesn't hurt anymore.

Healing isn't a destination.
I didn't realize that instantly —
More like a slow, deliberate unfolding.

Some mornings you wake up motivated
—
Hitting the gym, having a full breakfast,
journaling.
Other days, you don't even want to get
out of bed.

And that's okay. Healing isn't consistent,
But showing up for it every day is.

You don't need all the answers to be
healing.
You don't need to be "there" to be
growing.
Right now, you are becoming —
Even if you can't see it yet.

So, take a deep breath.
Let the world spin without you for a
moment.
And remember:

You are allowed to be a work in progress.
You are allowed to still be figuring it out.

So, what are you still figuring out?

(Use this Space)

If you are Reading this...

"Be kind to yourself"

Dear Reader,

These chapters may have triggered something in you — or maybe you loved them. That part is entirely up to you. You might have deeply resonated with some moments, and not at all with others. And that's okay.

I didn't pen this book expecting everyone to relate to every single word. I wrote it to reflect different views, different struggles — the quiet, messy, beautiful chaos that shapes each of our lives.

Maybe you're already deep into your healing journey.
Maybe you've just taken your first step.
Or maybe you're not sure if you even

want to begin,
or need to begin.

Wherever you are, I hope this book made you feel seen — even if just for a moment.
I hope it reminded you that healing doesn't have to be linear, loud, or perfect.

Above all, I hope it reminded you to be gentle with yourself.
You're allowed to take your time.
You're allowed to not have it all figured out.
And you are always — *always* — allowed to begin again.

With all my heart,
M. S

THANK YOU

www.ingramcontent.com/pod-product-compliance
Ingram Content Group UK Ltd.
Pitfield, Milton Keynes, MK11 3LW, UK
UKHW041311190726
13845UKWH00025B/200

9 789355 923721